MW01245852

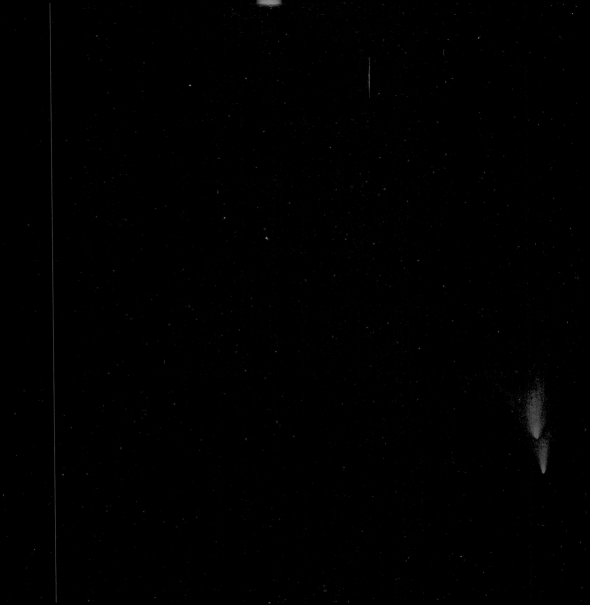

REGARDLESS OF WHAT CAME BEFORE
OR OF WHAT HAS YET TO COME, WHAT
MATTERS MOST RIGHT NOW IS HOW I
CHOOSE TO RESPOND TO THE
CHALLENGE BEFORE ME. WILL I LIE DOWN
OR WILL I FIGHT? THE CHOICE IS MINE
AND I CHOOSE TO FINISH STRONG.

DAN GREEN

FINISH STRONG

STRONG

TEEN ATHLETE

by Dan Green

www.simpletruths.com
Toll Free 800-900-3427

Book Design: Vieceli Design Company,
West Dundee, Illinois

Editing by Alice Patenaude

PHOTO CREDITS:
Getty Images: pages 6, 14, 19, 38, 55, 62, 60-61,
65, 66, 74, 82, 90, 97, 111, 120, 137
Corbis: pages 30, 31, 57
Derek Molis: page 100
All other images images courtesy iStockphoto.com.

04 WOZ 13

TABLE OF CONTENTS

KEEP COMING BACK, AND THOUGH THE
WORLD MAY ROMP ACROSS YOUR SPINE,
LET EVERY GAME'S END FIND YOU
STILL UPON THE BATTLING LINE;
FOR WHEN THE ONE GREAT SCORER
COMES TO MARK AGAINST YOUR NAME,
HE WRITES—NOT THAT YOU WON OR LOST—
BUT HOW YOU PLAYED THE GAME.

— GRANTLAND RICE

INTRODUCTION

You're an athlete. You live for the final shot, the sprint to the finish line, a chance to make the game-saving tackle or to score the winning touchdown. The rush of adrenaline and the thrill of victory are your rewards for years of training. You're an athlete, and you're reading this book for a reason. Maybe your coach gave it to you, maybe a friend loaned it to you or maybe someone that cares about you gave it to you as a gift. Either way, I suspect you gravitated toward the title because you know how important it is to **FINISH STRONG**—in sports, in school and most of all in life.

While researching these inspirational stories, I've discovered a pattern of core values that are present in many of the featured athletes. And over the past 20 years, I've successfully taken on many different roles—athlete, racecar driver, inventor, salesman, sales leader, sales trainer, author, husband and father. In each unique role, I had to learn to apply the principles of this book in order to be successful. In the process, I've learned to live the best life I can for myself and my family. Indeed, the process continues today. I'm constantly practicing the principles outlined in this book in my day-to-day life. It never ends. You must continually challenge yourself to grow or you risk dying on the vine.

The stories collected here are related to my life philosophy and to my vision expressed in my original book, *FINISH STRONG*, to raise a call to action. To live the **FINISH STRONG** attitude,

PLAY LIKE
YOU'RE IN
FIRST,
BUT TRAIN
LIKE YOU'RE
IN SECOND.

you must explore, understand and embrace the core values outlined in each of the chapters. As an athlete, you must strive to carry out these principles each and every day. If you do so, you will position yourself for success in your athletic endeavors. And most importantly, in doing so, you are "practicing" for the game of life. The core values that you develop as a teen athlete will become the underpinnings of your life's values—positioning you for greater success in LIFE.

As you read through *FINISH STRONG*, take time to stop and think about each principle. What can you take away from the stories that will help you become a better athlete and individual?

The champion's questions and thoughts are offered to inspire you to develop your own positive voice. Read them carefully, understand the meaning and then strive to create your own internal voice. Think of these questions and thoughts as golden nuggets. Then use these nuggets to create your own golden masterpiece.

Your teenage years will be some of the most challenging, frustrating, fun-filled and rewarding years of your life. But it is also in these years that you are casting the mold for the person you will become.

I challenge you to not treat this time in your life lightly. You have an amazing opportunity to "set your sails" in life for a wonderful journey. Use your time wisely to set your goals, practice smart, train hard, be a leader, study and make sure that you finish each day strong. Resolve today to **FINISH STRONG** in all you do. Then, hold yourself accountable to that resolution. If you'll do this, I guarantee you that your life will be more rewarding than you ever imagined.

So let's get started!

Dan

Dan Green

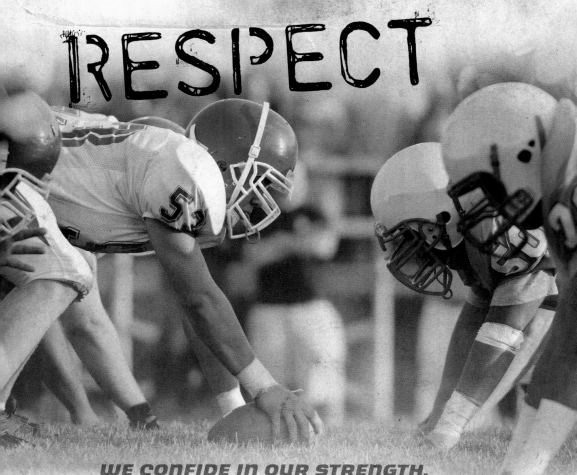

RESPECT

**WE CONFIDE IN OUR STRENGTH,
WITHOUT BOASTING OF IT; WE RESPECT
THAT OF OTHERS, WITHOUT FEARING IT.**
—Thomas Jefferson

YOU GOTTA LOSE 'EM SOMETIMES. WHEN YOU DO, LOSE 'EM RIGHT.

– CASEY STENGEL

Winning graciously is easy. Dignified defeat is difficult. In fact, sometimes the greatest respect is earned by the way you respond when your opponent has outplayed you.

Respect isn't given. IT'S EARNED.

Respect means more than just playing hard and playing fair. Respect begins with a higher awareness of yourself, your team-mates, your opponents, your coaches and your sport as you become the kind of player that everyone wants on their team. Respect is important in all aspects of life, and it is essential in sports.

RESPECT

Underestimating the strength, skill and talents of your competition is a lack of respect that can bite you hard. Very rarely do you hear a winning team say they "really overestimated the other team's abilities." But respect runs deeper than the field of competition. It's about understanding that your opponent is made of flesh and blood just like you. We all share a common denominator and showing respect for this fact is **essential in becoming an athlete of significance.**

A CHAMPION ASKS...

WHO IS MY COMPETITION?

WHAT ARE THEY GOOD AT?

HOW CAN I LOSE TO THEM?

SARA TUCHOLSKY

RESPECT

WILL CARRY YOU HOME

Western Oregon University's Sara Tucholsky had no idea that the first—and, as it turns out, only—home run of her career would cause ripples that would make her last swing of the bat as a college softball player, a national media sensation.

With two runners on and her team down a run to Central Washington University, Sara hit a home run to centerfield. As she rounded first base, she missed the bag. When she turned to tag the base, she injured her knee. Able only to crawl back to the base, Sara was told that she would be called out if her teammates came to her aid. If a pinch runner checked into the game, her home run would count only as a single.

14

3 FOR 34
ON THE SEASON

Players and fans alike were stunned when Central Washington first baseman Mallory Holtman, the conference's all-time home-run leader, asked the umpire if there was any rule against opponents helping an injured player around the bases.

She was told that there was not. Together, Holtman and shortstop Liz Wallace picked up Tucholsky and carried her around the bases, stopping at each bag to allow Sara to touch it with her good leg.

"It was the right thing to do,"

Holtman said in an interview on national television, after the respectful act of sportsmanship had been witnessed by millions on ESPN and had become a internet sensation.

The three runs sent Western Oregon to a 4-2 victory, ending Central Washington's chances of winning the conference and advancing to the playoffs.

"It's a great story," Western Oregon coach Pam Knox said, "something I'll never forget—the game's about character and integrity and sportsmanship, and it's not always about winning and losing."

As it turns out, the players who helped Sara had no idea of the circumstances surrounding the at-bat, or that the story would make headlines around the country. "We didn't know that she was a senior or that this was her first home run," Wallace said Wednesday. "That makes the story more touching than it was. We just wanted to help her." The gesture left Sara's Western Oregon teammates in tears. "I hope I would do the same for her in the same situation," Sara said. Central Washington coach Gary Frederick called the act of sportsmanship, "Unbelievable."

"In the end, it is not about winning and losing so much," Holtman, who initiated the act, said. "It was about this girl. She hit it over the fence and was in pain, and she deserved a home run."

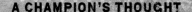

A CHAMPION'S THOUGHT

JACKIE ROBINSON
★★★ PROFESSIONAL BASEBALL PLAYER ★★★
WORLD SERIES CHAMPION, SIX-TIME ALL-STAR

I'm not concerned with your liking
or disliking me. All I ask is that you
respect me as a human being.

17

ENTHUSIASM

DO YOU KNOW WHAT MY FAVORITE PART OF THE GAME IS? THE OPPORTUNITY TO PLAY.

— Mike Singletary

ENTHUSIASM IS CONTAGIOUS.

Ask Mike Singletary, the anchor of a 1986 Chicago Bears defense that still ranks as one of the NFL's best ever. Known for his intense gaze across the line of scrimmage, Singletary epitomized the athlete whose love of the sport rubbed off on anyone who ever saw him play.

What is enthusiasm? When the Pittsburgh Steelers' Troy Polamalu appears from nowhere with improbable speed and makes a touchdown-saving tackle. Or the Cleveland Cavaliers' LeBron James gets the crowd to their feet with one of his many highlight dunks.

Enthusiasm is a deeply held love of the sport

that's made stronger every time you feel the rush of adrenaline, the thrill of competition, the joy of a game well played.

IT'S WHEN YOU FEEL LUCKY JUST TO HAVE
THE OPPORTUNITY
⊙ TO COMPETE. ⊙

Sometimes, though, enthusiasm can be measured not by what you've accomplished, but by how you respond when things don't go your way. Your ability to keep your fire burning in the midst of a storm is paramount to becoming a champion. In addition, your ability to recognize a weakness, accept it and move past it, is a critical characteristic of building and maintaining your enthusiasm.

ONE MAN PRACTICING SPORTSMANSHIP IS FAR BETTER THAN 50 PREACHING IT. — KNUTE K. ROCKNE

A CHAMPION ASKS...

DOES MY ENTHUSIASM SHINE THROUGH EVEN IN TOUGH TIMES?

AM I A LEADER IN INSPIRING OTHERS?

IS MY ATTITUDE CONTAGIOUS AND IS IT WORTH CATCHING?

21

ENTHUSIASM
KNOWS NO BOUNDARIES
CULLEN FITZGIBBONS

Los Alamitos High School wrestler Cullen Fitzgibbons has a record that very few athletes would envy: 0-28, winless in four years of bouts. Cullen never made the varsity team, and sometimes opposing wrestlers would take it easy on him, knowing that he had little chance of beating them.

Despite what others might see as failure, **Cullen never missed a practice, never complained about his lack of success, never passed up a chance to root his teammates on to victory.** Cullen has Down syndrome. And on an evening in March 2008, Cullen was recognized as the "Inspirational Wrestler of the Year" at California's state finals. His mother summed up years of support and the fight to get Cullen into regular classrooms, where he could inspire others with his

0-28

infectious enthusiasm. **"It was surreal watching this entire arena giving my son a standing ovation,"** Dana Fitzgibbons said. **"They were all saluting him. It was powerful."**

Enthusiasm comes from the heart, and in a wrestling career in which Cullen never had the referee raise his hand in victory, he seized the opportunities given to him and embraced the moments when he could transcend his limitations.

Cullen's father, Billy, was a top college wrestler himself and aspired to the U.S. Olympic team. Having a son who could never follow in his footsteps might have devastated him. But Cullen's enthusiasm has given his father renewed purpose.

"I cried when I found out he had Down syndrome," Billy Fitzgibbons said. **"I didn't see what the future was going to hold. And now the future; it's nothing I could've imagined. It's so sweet."**

A CHAMPION'S THOUGHT

★★★ **BABE RUTH** ★★★

MAJOR LEAGUE LEGEND, SEVEN-TIME WORLD SERIES
CHAMPION, HOME RUN LEADER FOR 39 YEARS

The most important thing that young athletes must do is to pick the right sport. Not one that they just like a little bit but one that they love because, if they don't really love their sport, they won't work as hard as they should. Me? I loved to hit.

COMMITMENT

ONCE YOU MAKE A DECISION, THE UNI-VERSE CONSPIRES TO MAKE IT HAPPEN.

— Ralph Waldo Emerson

You don't have to be a world-class athlete to understand the value of commitment. Commitment is one of the most important attributes any athlete can possess, a promise that you make to yourself to follow through—to continue in the face of adversity, to reach your goals despite the inevitable hardships. Plenty of talented athletes fail. Why? Because without commitment, success is impossible.

COMMITMENT ISN'T A GOAL; IT'S A WAY OF LIFE.

1	Wk 9	5/3/09 (Thurs)		Report to sch	Poly
		7/3/09 (Sat)	8am 8.15am 9-12pm 12.30pm	Leave for NP Training at NP gym (with 144 mats) Back to SHPS for dismissal	
2					School Hall
		10/3/09 (Tue)	3.30 – 5.30pm		School Hall
3	Wk 10				Ngee Ann Poly
		12/3/09 (Thurs)	3.30 – 5.30pm		
4		14/3/09 (Sat)	8am 8.15am 4.15pm	Report to sch Leave for NP Training at NP gym (with 144 mats) SHPS for dismissal	

27

An important key to commitment is accountability. Have you openly expressed your goals to others? Or have you hidden them within yourself? Ultimately, you have to perform for yourself and hold yourself accountable, but there is something very powerful about verbalizing a goal and making it clear to your friends and family. Your level of commitment increases through your accountability to others.

Take your commitment to the next level by letting others in on your goals.

Write your goals on paper and constantly remind yourself of the benefits of reaching your goals. That's **FINISH STRONG** Commitment.

KEYS TO SETTING GOALS

1. BE SPECIFIC ABOUT WHAT YOU WANT.

2. IT MUST BE MEASURABLE.

3. IT MUST BE REALISTIC AND ATTAINABLE.

4. THE GOAL MUST BE RELEVANT.

5. IT MUST BE TIME-BOUND.

> GOALS DETERMINE WHAT YOU'RE GOING TO BE.
> ---JULIUS ERVING

A CHAMPION ASKS...

AM I MORE COMMITTED TO MY ACTIONS TODAY THAN YESTERDAY?

AM I "ALL-IN"?

HOW CAN I RE-AFFIRM MY COMMITMENT ON A DAILY BASIS?

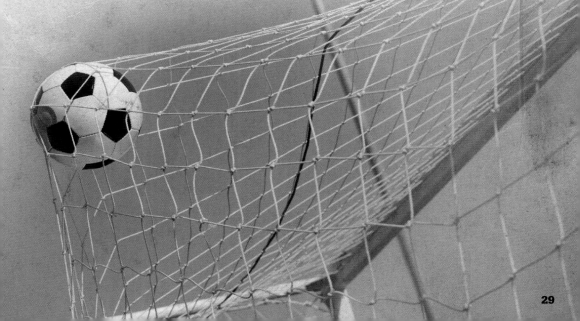

COMMITMENT

TO SPEED AHEAD

Football fans remember Renaldo Nehemiah as the track star who traded on his speed to become a wide receiver —one of the fastest in the NFL—for the San Francisco 49ers in the early 1980s. The highlight of Nehemiah's career was his team's victory over the Miami Dolphins in Super Bowl XIX.

But before he ever put on the pads, Nehemiah was a high-school hurdling legend in his native New Jersey. Despite his slight build—at 5'8" and 150 pounds, he wasn't the largest athlete on the track—he was the first (and still the only) high-school athlete to break 13 seconds for the 100-meter hurdles, a race that he ran because it was one of the most demanding—and the most intimidating. **"Everyone else was afraid of 'em," Nehemiah said of the hurdles. "I was fast, but really, I did it on a dare. I was enamored with the ability to run and jump at the same time. It made me feel special."**

42 vs. 39

How dominant was Nehemiah when he stepped on the track?

During his sophomore year, after suffering a torn hamstring that nearly ended his promising career, **Nehemiah re-committed himself to becoming the best prep hurdler in the country.**

By the following season, Coach Jean Poquette routinely insisted his star clear 42-inch hurdles—3 inches higher than the rest of the field in the 110-meter race, because he knew that Nehemiah would be running the higher hurdles when he exploded onto the college track scene.

Even willingly handicapped by the higher hurdle, Nehemiah didn't lose. "I wasn't a fan of those workouts initially," he said of the work ethic instilled in him by Poquette, who included runs with the middle-distance athletes in Nehemiah's conditioning.

"Coach used to say practice would be hard, and the races would be easy. My mindset was that nobody else in my event was as strong as I was."

It was his early commitment to training and the ability to push himself to extraordinary degrees that led Nehemiah to professional success.

ONCE CLEARED, A SINGLE HURDLE—NO MATTER HOW HIGH—WILL ALWAYS BE BEHIND YOU.

VINCE LOMBARDI

NFL COACH, FIVE-TIME NFL CHAMPION AND
★★ TWO-TIME SUPER BOWL CHAMPION ★★

A man can be as great as he wants to be. If you believe in yourself and have the courage, the deter— mination, the dedication, the competitive drive and if you are willing to sacrifice the little things in life and pay the price for the things that are worthwhile, it can be done. Once a man has made a commitment to a way of life, he puts the greatest strength in the world behind him. It's something we call "heart power." Once a man has made this commitment, nothing will stop him short of success.

COMMIT

PRIORITIES

DECIDE WHAT YOU WANT. DECIDE WHAT YOU ARE WILLING TO EXCHANGE FOR IT. ESTABLISH YOUR PRIORITIES AND GO TO WORK.

— H. L. Hunt

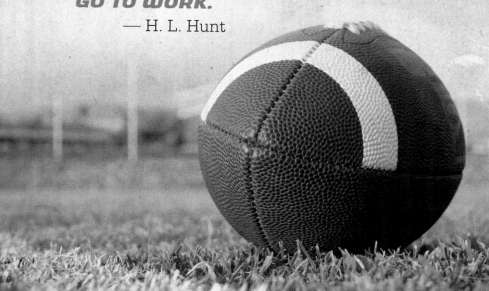

I challenge you to stop and think at this moment:

"IS READING THIS BOOK THE BEST USE OF YOUR TIME?"

I hope that your answer is yes. But why?

PRIORITY 4

PRIORITY 3

PRIORITY 2

PRIORITY 1

What is the return you are expecting for reading this book? Maybe you're looking for some positive inspiration before game time. Maybe you're reading this book just before bedtime so that your subconscious will soak up the inspirational message, or maybe you are in-between classes and need to "kill a few minutes." There is some reason that you have chosen to read this book at this moment. In doing so, you've made a conscious effort to put off doing anything else. The time you spend right now can never be recaptured. You've placed a high priority on this effort relative to your other "to-dos."

EVERY PASSION HAS ITS DESTINY.

Setting priorities is critical in reaching your goals in life, school and sports. Without priorities your days can be wasted running from one task to another. You will become frustrated, agitated and most likely fail more often than not. There's an old Chinese proverb that fits, "If you chase two rabbits, they both will escape." Don't get caught chasing two rabbits.

Take time to plan your approach to reaching your goals.

Prioritize your tasks and commit to focusing on your priorities, one at a time. Once you've done this, you will find that you will be freer to concentrate on the task at hand; consequently leading to a more successful outcome in all you do.

Many books have been written about goal setting and time management: Sean Covey's *The Seven Habits of Highly Effective Teens* is one of the best. If you've not already done so, I encourage you to find a copy, read it and put it to work for you. This should be your next priority!

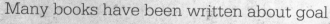

PRIORITIES
1. Keep training.
2. Eat right.
3. Get enough sleep.
4. Excel in school.
5. Be the best.

A CHAMPION ASKS...

HOW DO I WANT TO BE REMEMBERED WHEN I'M GONE?

WHAT'S THE BEST USE OF MY TIME RIGHT NOW?

CAN I COMMIT 100% OF MY FOCUS TO THE TASK AT HAND?

37

TIM TEBOW

PRIORITIES

MAKE A DIFFERENCE

In 2007, as a sophomore quarterback at the University of Florida, Tim Tebow took college football by storm, becoming **the first underclassman to win the coveted Heisman Trophy** as the nation's best player. In 2009, Tebow led his Gators to yet another National Championship.

Even those who didn't know Tim or who rooted against his Gators respected the way he handled himself during the season. His humble attitude and focus on teamwork won him fans from around the country.

His 6'2", 240-pound body—more like that of a linebacker than a quarterback—instilled fear in opposing defenses. They'd gotten a taste of what they were in for during Tim's freshman season when he took the opportunity that Coach

Urban Meyer gave him, running and passing for a touchdown during the 2006 BCS National Championship game against Ohio State. His Gators prevailed 49-14.

It was not only a big win for UF, but a chance for Tim to show that he was ready to take over the quarterbacking duties from Gators' veteran Chris Leak. Tim's known for a hard-nosed style that finds him in the middle of—and often running through— an overmatched defense. He was the first player in college football history to run for 20 touchdowns and pass for 20 touchdowns. He finished the 2007 season with 3,970 yards of total offense and accounted for 51 of the team's touchdowns.

"I am fortunate, fortunate for a lot of things," Tim said in his speech at the New York Athletic Club, where he accepted the Heisman, one of a handful of major awards he won for his efforts. "God truly blessed me and this just adds on. It's an honor. I'm so happy to be here."

By his sophomore year in college, Tebow would already be one of the most honored football players in college history. But it wasn't always this way—not by a long shot. Tim grew up in Ponte Vedra Beach, Florida, near Jacksonville, and played football at Nease High School. But he was never a student there. Instead, he was homeschooled by his mother. Tim's parents, Bob and Pam, were Christian missionaries in the Philippines when Tim was born, and they always placed a strong emphasis on family values and hard work.

He was a good student, but it was Tim's skills on the football field that drew interest from many Division I programs. They liked his talent—and they loved his toughness and his character. Tim, they knew, made the most of every opportunity on and off the football field to make good decisions.

Despite his tremendous success, though, Tim keeps his role as an athlete in perspective.

Football remains just one of several important things in his life. In fact, he places football fourth on his list of priorities, behind faith, family and academics. Everywhere and always he seeks out opportunities to lead by serving others. Tim joins his father on mission trips to the Philippines, where he visits orphanages, medical clinics, hospitals, prisons and schools. "Every time you go, you learn something different," Tim said, "and it changes your life even more."

While many other college students are vacationing in Daytona Beach, Florida, or on a beach in Mexico, Tim sees spring break as an opportunity to help others. Coach Meyer encourages his players' interest in doing the right thing, Tim said.

"He's one of the best coaches in college football, but he's more than that."

Balancing his opportunities on the football field with the other opportunities in his life has made Tim Tebow successful in everything he does.

"There are more important things in life than winning football games," Tim said. "The way you treat people is going to last forever. . . . **When it's all said and done, people aren't going to remember how many championships you won, they're going to remember what you were like off the field, how you treated people."**

41

★★ NANCY LOPEZ ★★
PROFESSIONAL GOLFER, 48 PROFESSIONAL WINS
WITH THREE MAJOR CHAMPIONSHIPS

When I had to give up swimming because it wasn't good for my golfing muscles, I began to think of what else I would have to sacrifice if I wanted to keep playing golf. In the years between 10 and 13, I gave up many things just so I could play golf.

RISK

PLAY THE GAME FOR MORE THAN YOU CAN AFFORD TO LOSE ... ONLY THEN WILL YOU LEARN THE GAME.

— Winston Churchill

A CROSSING ROUTE in football is a relatively easy play to run and it's a great play to gain short yardage.

If you're not familiar with this play, let me explain. It begins with the receiver starting from one end of the field, advancing forward for five to ten yards and then making a horizontal cut toward the center of the field and through the heart of the defense.

It's a timing play that the quarterback and receiver have most likely practiced hundreds of times. The perfect pass will hit the receiver square in the chest, allowing him to quickly protect the football and make a move down the field. However, if the pass is thrown even a bit too high, it forces the receiver to make a split-second decision. Does he reach out to catch the pass in order to make the play or not? On the surface, it sounds like a no-brainer. Go for it, right? Not so fast. Here's the risk that the player must assess: If he reaches out, he leaves himself completely exposed to a crushing tackle, pain and possible injury. In this

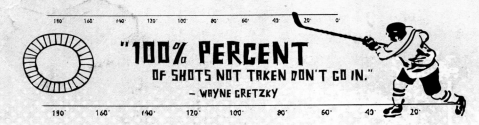

"100% PERCENT OF SHOTS NOT TAKEN DON'T GO IN."
– WAYNE GRETZKY

split second, the receiver must take all matters into account in order to calculate the risk of making such a move and then compare this risk to the potential reward of making the catch and gaining the yardage. Is the pass actually catchable? How close is the defense? How healthy is he? Can his body take a hit? How bad will it hurt? What will his coach and teammates think if he doesn't try?

It's not surprising that many times receivers do not fully commit to taking on the risk and, as a result, they don't make the catch. There's a known syndrome in football to explain this phenomenon and it's called "Alligator Arms," or the inability to reach out and make the play. The next time you need to take a risk in order to reach out to achieve your goal, don't get "Alligator Arms." Don't be afraid to go out on a limb. After all, that's where all the fruit is.

IN THE LONG RUN, YOU HIT ONLY WHAT YOU AIM AT.
— HENRY DAVID THOREAU

A CHAMPION ASKS ...

HAVE OTHERS OVERCOME THIS RISK BEFORE?

IS THE REWARD WORTH THE RISK?

HOW CAN I MINIMIZE THE RISK AND MAXIMIZE THE REWARD?

49

RISK

TO JUMP IN THE DEEP END

ANDREW LUK

Andrew Luk will never win an Olympic medal, but that doesn't stop him from competing against other swimmers who have a huge advantage—the gift of sight. Andrew is blind. In 2008, he made the junior varsity swim team as a sophomore at Diamond Bar High School in California. He gets around his high school campus with the aid of a cane. His laptop translates his school work into Braille.

Teachers and counselors encouraged him to give swimming a shot, so he decided to give it his all and compete in the 500-meter freestyle. He explained his decision this way:

"It was a need to be part of something and get out and do something I enjoyed, because for a long time I've been sitting around and talking about what my future could hold, but never got up and did anything."

Though he would like to be, of course, he's not the fastest swimmer in the pool. It's not unusual for Andrew to finish alone, a couple of laps behind faster opponents. It's also not unusual for members of rival teams to stop whatever they are doing and line the pool to cheer Andrew on to the finish. "It's been the most touching thing, the opposing team coming up and congratulating me and complimenting me and telling me that I've inspired them," Andrew said. But it's not Andrew's times that impress teammates and opponents, despite the fact that his performance has steadily improved (by more than a minute in one three-race stretch).

No, it's his willingness to take on an unnatural risk and to turn a disadvantage into an inspiration, a shining example of what hard work and dedication can do. It leaves those watching in awe, and even fans from rival schools chanting for Andrew to finish—and applauding him when he does.

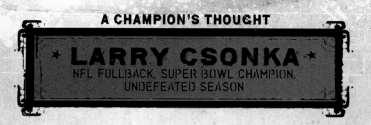

★ **LARRY CSONKA** ★

NFL FULLBACK, SUPER BOWL CHAMPION,
UNDEFEATED SEASON

Any time you try to win everything, you must be willing to lose everything.

RISK

THE INNER VOICE

By Derek Molis

Every athlete has an inner voice of pride. It is the voice only athletes can hear, pushing them to the brink of exhaustion, demanding excellence and condemning failure. Failure, understand, is the driving force behind an athlete. Every athlete has experienced failure, and now trains so he or she will not experience it again. This inner voice knows the difference between training and exercising. Many athletes exercise, stopping when they have reached a perceived limit, or when it becomes uncomfortable to continue. But only a select few athletes have the heart and desire to train unconditionally. Only a select few push past their physical and mental limits. Only a select few push past the pain and discomfort. Only a select few have the courage and the character to understand that training makes them quicker, faster, stronger, but most importantly, allows them to gain a mental edge over future opponents. So when failure laughs in my face as I desperately try and earn the respect of that last repetition, it must realize one thing: Each time I train, I not only hear, but I answer the Inner Voice.

PASSION

I WANT TO BE REMEMBERED AS THE GUY WHO GAVE HIS ALL WHENEVER HE WAS ON THE FIELD.

— Walter Payton

Passion can be instilled in you by parents or mentors or friends. But for passion to burn hot enough to push you to succeed, it's got to come from inside. No one else can will you to be passionate about sports or the cornerstone events in your life. No one but you can make the sacrifices that will allow you to get the most out of your talent.

Enthusiasm provides the energy, but passion provides the emotion.

When you combine the two, then great things are possible. You will **FINISH STRONG!**

So be honest with yourself. What really drives you through adversity? What genuinely makes you happy? What causes the pit of your stomach to turn with excitement? Take the time to reflect on these questions and keep your passion burning bright.

A CHAMPION ASKS...

 AM I GIVING MY BEST AT THIS VERY MOMENT?

 DOES MY PASSION SHINE THROUGH?

 HOW MUCH MORE CAN I GIVE?

PASSION

TO SUCCEED

PISTOL PETE

"Pistol" Pete Maravich was one of the most electrifying college players of all time, averaging more than 44 points a game over his career at Louisiana State University, and garnering three All-America honors before moving on to an all-star career in the NBA.

44
POINTS PER
GAME OVER
PETE'S CAREER

The stories of Pete's dedication to the game are the stuff of legend. By the age of 7, on the courts of Aliquippa, Pennsylvania, a small suburb of Pittsburgh, he would sleep with his basketball (a practice he continued into high school), rolling the ball off his fingertips until he nodded off from exhaustion. Often, he would practice six to 10 hours a day during the summer, working on the ball skills that would delight crowds and confuse opponents.

Part of Pete's motivation came from his father, Press Maravich, a former professional player and later a coach, who encouraged Pete to work for a college scholarship—an award that would mean a great deal both to Pete and the family.

"I'd never heard anything like that," Pete said of his father's pep talks, which fueled the boy's passion.

"I wanted that, more than anything in the world, and so from that time on I began a very strict commitment to basketball. Basketball became my God. **There was nothing else that could enter into my life.** My goals were already set, short term and long term. And there was never a doubt in my mind that one day I would play professional basketball, make a million dollars, and be on a team that won the world championship."

His father challenged young Pete by requiring that he make 100 free throws after dinner before he could go back into the house to get ready for bed. Pete, who rarely missed, made the exercises even more grueling by making all but the last shot before missing on purpose so that he could stay outside longer and hone his skills.

Pete was a standout at high schools in North Carolina and South Carolina, earning the nickname **"Pistol Pete"** from a quirky shooting style developed over the years. Highly recruited to some of the country's best colleges, Pete instead decided to play for his father, who was coaching at the time at LSU. **During his time at LSU, he scored 3,667 points and averaged 44 points per game**—an NCAA Division I record that stands to this day and without the benefit of the three-point line.

Despite being overshadowed later by the superstars in an NBA that had become more commercial, Pete's ten-year career (1970-1980) still places him among the best ever to play the game. In 1996, he was named one of the 50 Greatest Players in NBA History.

Few would argue that anyone has ever surpassed his passion for basketball.

A CHAMPION'S THOUGHT

PEGGY FLEMMING

FIGURE SKATER, THREE-TIME WORLD CHAMPION
★★★ & OLYMPIC GOLD MEDALIST ★★★

The most important thing is to love your sport. Never do it to please someone else—it has to be yours. That is all that will justify the hard work needed to achieve success. Compete against yourself, not others, for that is who is truly your best competition.

PASSION

COURAGE

COURAGE IS ALMOST A CONTRADICTION IN TERMS. IT MEANS A STRONG DESIRE TO LIVE TAKING THE FORM OF A READINESS TO DIE.

— Gilbert K. Chesterton

Courage is a term that can instantly create visions of a soldier charging a hill or a fireman saving a child from a burning building. These are heroic images that involve risking life and limb. And each of these images involves a decision made by an individual to overcome the natural fear of death in order to help someone else. As an athlete, the risk of death in most prep sports is marginal. But that doesn't mean that you have no reason to fear. Nor does it mean that courage is not required to do what you do.

PLAY FEARLESS
5

Courage is not the absence of fear. On the contrary, courage cannot exist without the presence of fear. It is your acceptance of fear and your commitment to moving toward your objective that reveals courage. Whether you are facing the state champion in your next wrestling match, or you're lining up against a defensive end that weighs 40 pounds more than you, at some

point in your athletic life you will need to face your fear, accept it and keep moving forward. That is what courage is all about.

A CHAMPION ASKS...

 IS THERE A LEGITIMATE BASIS FOR MY FEAR?

 WHAT'S THE WORSE THING THAT CAN HAPPEN?

 WHAT IS THE BENEFIT TO OVER-COMING MY FEAR?

BETHANY HAMILTON
COURAGE
TO FACE YOUR FEARS

It was a perfect day for surfing off the coast of Kauai. A 13-year-old surfing protégé had just finished riding a 20-foot wave and was lying face down on her surf board. Preparing to paddle out to catch another wave, her thoughts of becoming a professional surfer shifted in an instant. Without warning, she felt a tug on her left arm and in a split second she realized that she'd been attacked by a shark. As she struggled to gain her composure she realized something even more horrifying—the 14-foot tiger shark had bit clean through her board, taking her left arm in a single bite. At that moment in time, survival, not surfing, became her priority.

Bethany Hamilton learned to surf at the age of 4. When she

was 8, she entered her first contest and won both of the events she competed in. At the age of 10, she placed 1st in the "11-under girls," 1st in the "15-under girls," and 2nd in the "12-under boys" division at the Volcom Puffer-Fish contest. She was determined to become a professional surfer and was certainly on track to make it happen. Then, in one violently swift moment on that fall day in 2003, it seemed her dreams would be shattered.

However, Bethany was born with the heart of a lion and the competitive spirit of a thoroughbred. She was determined to surf again. With the support of her friends and family, and her faith in

God, Bethany recovered rapidly, and within **only ten weeks of the attack, she returned to the water.** Convinced she could overcome her physical challenge, she worked hard to learn to surf

with her disability. Moreover, she also had to overcome the psychological fear of another attack. Bethany would face her fears by singing and praying when she was out on the water.

Incredible as it seems, less than a year after her attack, Bethany returned to competition—taking fifth place at the National Surfing Championships and first place at the first event for the Hawaii National Scholastic Surfing Association. In 2004 ESPN awarded her the ESPY for "Best Comeback Athlete" of the year.

Bethany's ability to overcome her physical and mental challenges puts her in an elite class of achievers. Her unique ability to confront her fears, embrace them and then continue moving forward in the direction of her goals, is the perfect definition of courage.

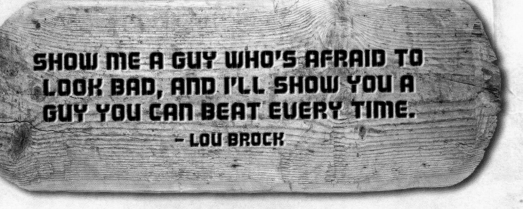

SHOW ME A GUY WHO'S AFRAID TO LOOK BAD, AND I'LL SHOW YOU A GUY YOU CAN BEAT EVERY TIME.
– LOU BROCK

RALPH WALDO EMERSON

★★★ ★★★

AMERICAN POET

Whatever you do, you need courage.
Whatever course you decide upon, there is
always someone to tell you that you are wrong.
There are always difficulties arising which
tempt you to believe that your critics are right.
To map out a course of action and follow it
requires some of the same courage which a
soldier needs. Peace has its victories, but it
takes a brave soul to win them.

COURAGE

GOALS

LIFE TAKES ON MEANING WHEN YOU BECOME MOTIVATED, SET GOALS AND CHARGE AFTER THEM IN AN UNSTOPPABLE MANNER.

— Les Brown

As an athlete, you set goals. To run faster, jump higher, score more often. Some goals are meant to be fulfilled quickly; others may take you a lifetime. The size of your goals isn't important. The important thing is that you set them and that you do whatever it takes to achieve them. Goals shove you toward your dreams. They nudge you when you feel sluggish. Goals force you to focus on moving forward when the easiest thing to do is watch from the sidelines. Without goals, athletes lack direction. The only thing hard work will do if you don't have a goal is to get you nowhere fast.

Win the game, educate others, live life to the fullest. Well-defined goals are the cornerstone of your success. It's up to you to know what you want—and to set the surest path to reach your goals as you strive to **FINISH STRONG**.

The trouble with not having a goal is that you can spend your life running up and down the field and never scoring. — Bill Copeland

A CHAMPION ASKS...

 ARE MY GOALS CURRENT?

 ARE MY GOALS REASONABLE?

 ARE MY GOALS PRIORITIZED?

GOALS
TO SWING FOR THE FENCES

April 11, 2008. Freedom vs. Aliquippa. A baseball game played in front of fewer than two dozen fans. The still photograph of John Challis at-bat doesn't tell the complete story of John's courage and character. In that picture, John, a Pittsburgh area teen who, at 5'6" and weighing 93 pounds, wears a flak jacket around his midsection for protection. From a pitcher's stand-point, he didn't present a menacing stature.

But the result speaks volumes to the importance of setting goals: the level swing, the solid contact, the hit between first and second base, and the jubilation of a young man who just two years before had been diagnosed with a disease that would eventually take his life. "First pitch, fastball. Right down the middle. I swing, I crack it … I get about 10 steps from the bag, and I'm screaming 'I did it! I did it,'" John said in an ESPN video tribute that aired on the afternoon of his passing in August 2008.

Such a simple thing as a base hit, an act repeated thousands of times every spring afternoon on baseball diamonds across the country. But for John Challis, it was the one goal that he had yet to fulfill in his life, a brief 18 years that came to an end even as he looked forward in the face of a seemingly impossible challenge.

One at-bat, one game, one more day is all he asked for. "He just wanted to prove to himself that he could do it," his father, Scott, said through tears.

"That must have been a good feeling for him to know, that's my boy, that's my boy who just got that hit," John said, imagining how his own success must have felt to a father who faced the loss of his only son. "Overcoming every odd there is … he's doing it. I couldn't live the rest of my life knowing that cancer got the best of me."

How tough was John Challis during his last days? The previous fall, he put on a football uniform for the final time against rival Hickory. He played on the kickoff team and lined up at wide receiver for a couple of plays, just because "I wanted to hit one last person." John's selfless attitude toward others even as the disease spread and doctors gave him only months to live was an inspiration to a region where sports and life are often intertwined. "If you don't get the results of your prayers, it isn't because God isn't answering them," John said. **"You need to open your eyes and see the greater picture … It makes you realize that seeing things in a positive manner affects more than just you."** The lesson? Sometimes our goals aren't God's goals. John's teammates organized, "Walk for a Champion," so that he could go on a final vacation with his family. While John graciously accepted the gesture, he insisted that any money left over be given to a family in need.

Before his death, John had the opportunity to meet some of his sports heroes, including Pittsburgh hockey legend **Mario Lemieux**, Steelers' quarterback **Ben Roethlisberger** and New York Yankees' slugger **Alex Rodriguez**—professionals who appreciated John's extraordinary fight and knew how much his example meant to others. Written in block letters on the bill of his baseball cap was John's motto throughout his ordeal and a message for those who would face similar battles:

COURAGE + BELIEVE = LIFE.

That's a goal not just for a courageous baseball player facing the fight of his life, but for anyone who wants to **FINISH STRONG**.

★ STEVE GARVEY ★
MAJOR LEAGUE FIRST BASEMAN, TEN-TIME ALL-STAR AND FOUR-TIME GOLD GLOVE AWARD WINNER

You have to set the goals that are almost out of reach. If you set a goal that is attainable without much work or thought, you are stuck with something below your true talent and potential.

STRENGTH

> **"Strength does not come from physical capacity, it comes from an indomitable will."**
> — Mahatma Ghandi

One of the most popular sideshows at the circus has always been the strong man, the muscled giant who wows audiences by bending steel with his bare hands or lifting a car. Sure, the show is impressive. But strength is about a whole lot more than just muscle. Using only the human body—the tools that God gave us when we were born—athletes routinely perform amazing feats of strength, agility and speed.

The physical expression of strength can be an impressive display. But strength is much more than size and power. Lines from Ecclesiastes are some of the most often quoted in inspirational literature, "The race is not to the swift, nor the battle to the strong." So what is true strength?

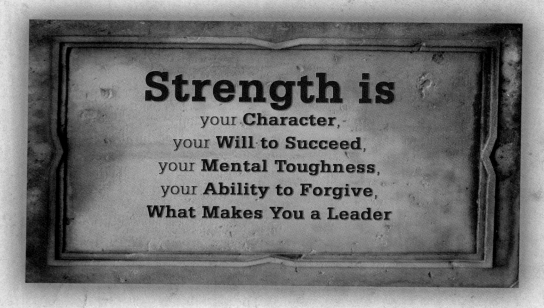

Strength is
your **Character**,
your **Will to Succeed**,
your **Mental Toughness**,
your **Ability to Forgive**,
What Makes You a Leader

Mahatma Ghandi said it well when he said, "Strength does not come from physical capacity, it comes from an indomitable will."

A CHAMPION ASKS...

WHAT CAN I ACCOMPLISH WITH WHAT I HAVE?

DO MY DAILY ACTIONS SUPPORT MY STRENGTH GOALS?

AM I GROWING STRONGER EACH DAY?

OSCAR PISTORIUS
STRENGTH

TO REMOVE BOUNDARIES

College athlete Oscar Pistorius is familiar to anybody who watched the 2008 Beijing Olympics—but not because he participated in them. A young South African sprinter, Oscar—known as the Blade Runner or "the fastest man on no legs"—attempted to qualify for the 400-meter race while running on "Cheetahs," two blades of carbon fiber that replace his lower legs.

Oscar was born without fibulas, the bone that runs from the knee to the ankle. When he was 11-months old, his legs were amputated below the knee. For most people, not having legs would stop them from participating in youth or high school sports, and certainly prevent them from harboring Olympic dreams. But not Oscar. As a boy, Oscar played water polo and tennis. A passionate rugby player, he took up sprinting as a teenager after being sidelined by an injury.

Imagine the audacity of such a thing. Would YOU have played sports had you no legs since birth? Would YOU have pushed forward with your athletic dreams? Well, Oscar sure did. Now a college student pursuing a degree in business management from the University of Pretoria, Oscar has since become one of the best sprinters in the world. Known as the **"FASTEST THING ON NO LEGS,"** Oscar's times would make any athlete jealous: 10.91 seconds for 100 meters, 21.58 for 200, and 46.34 for 400—all Paralympic world records. Good enough, in fact, that Pistorius petitioned the International Association of Athletics Federations (IAAF), track's world-governing body, to try to qualify for the 400-meter race in the Olympics. After fighting claims that he gained an advantage by running on the specially made blades, Oscar raced against the world's best runners, coming up just tenths of a second short of securing a spot on South Africa's Olympic track team. But that setback is nothing compared to what he's already accomplished through his strength and courage. Oscar couldn't have

10.91 seconds 100 meters

21.58 seconds 200 meters

46.34 seconds 400 meters

been happier to be given the chance to run against the world's best able-bodied sprinters.

Despite missing the qualifying time for the 2008 Olympics, Oscar has set his sights on the 2012 Olympics in London, England. He will be only 25, still in his prime as a sprinter. His chances to fulfill the dream are promising. Judging from the strength he's exhibited already, he'll be there.

THE DIFFERENCE BETWEEN A SUCCESSFUL PERSON AND OTHERS IS NOT A LACK OF STRENGTH, NOT A LACK OF KNOWLEDGE, BUT RATHER A LACK OF WILL.

-VINCENT T. LOMBARDI

RONALD REAGAN

40TH PRESIDENT OF THE UNITED STATES

The character that takes command in moments of crucial choices has already been determined. It has been determined by a thousand other choices made earlier in seemingly unimportant moments. It has been determined by all the little choices of years past—by all those times when the voice of conscience was at war with the voice of temptation, whispering the lie that it really doesn't matter. It has been determined by all the day—to—day decisions made when life seemed easy and crises seemed far away—the decisions that, piece by piece, bit by bit, developed habits of discipline or of laziness, habits of self—sacrifice or self—indulgence, habits of duty and honor and integrity—or dishonor and shame. Because, when life does get tough, and the crisis is undeniably at hand—when we must, in an instant, look inward for strength of character to see us through—we will find nothing inside ourselves that we have not already put there.

STRENGTH

OPPORTUNITY

"We are all faced with a series of great opportunities," Charles R. Swindoll said, **"brilliantly disguised as impossible situations."** Opportunity is a funny thing.

You say that someone presented with an opportunity is given a chance, but that makes it sound like luck is involved.

For athletes, opportunity only appears after you've put in the hard work, after you've dedicated yourself to the goal, after you've committed yourself to winning. **You have available to you all the resources that you need to succeed, but you are guaranteed nothing. The ability to smell and seize opportunity is the cornerstone of athletic success.**

Penn State football coach Joe Paterno, the winningest coach in Division I history, was an assistant under his predecessor, Rip Engle, for 16 seasons beginning in 1950. When given the opportunity to coach his first football team in 1966, Paterno made the most of it. In more than 40 years at the helm,

he's racked up nearly 400 wins, two national titles, and the respect of coaches, players, and fans around the country. "The will to win is important," Paterno said. "But the will to prepare is vital." Legendary University of Alabama football coach Paul "Bear" Bryant—the man Paterno passed with his 324th win—had a creed that he lived by and that he made sure his players followed: **know what's expected of you, and when you get an opportunity to perform, make the most of it.** Our world is full of opportunities. Henry Ford, the father of the automobile in America, said it best:

A generation ago there were
a thousand men to every
opportunity, while today there
are a thousand opportunities
to every man.

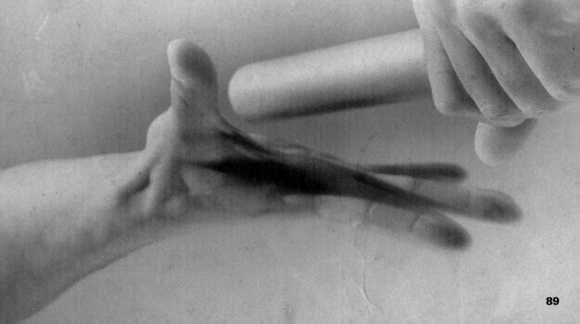

A CHAMPION ASKS...

 AM I WILLING TO STEP UP TO THE LINE WHEN OPPORTUNITY CALLS?

 WHAT CAN I DO AT THIS MOMENT TO PREPARE MYSELF FOR NEW OPPORTUNITIES?

 HOW CAN I CREATE NEW OPPORTUNITIES?

JASON MCELWAIN
OPPORTUNITY
TAKES A SHOT

Jason McElwain—"J-Mac" to his friends and teammates—was the much-loved manager of his suburban Rochester, New York, Greece Athena High School basketball team. Few people thought he would ever be more than that. **Jason is autistic, a condition that makes social interaction and communication difficult.** He knew that even if he practiced with the team and gave it his all, he probably wouldn't see much playing time. But on the night of February 16, 2006, something magical happened.

Coach Jim Johnson, recognizing the sacrifices that Jason had made as the team's manager, gave him a spot on the roster and suited him up with the rest of the players. With his team ahead comfortably, Coach Johnson brought Jason off the bench in the last four minutes of the game. After all, he had worked hard and deserved to be recognized for his role on the team.

No one in the gym was prepared for what they were about to witness. After missing his first two shots, Jason made six three-pointers and scored a total of 20 points. With each basket, fans cheered louder and louder until, at the final buzzer, the capacity crowd rushed the court, mobbing Jason and congratulating him on his amazing performance.

6 THREE-POINTERS

"This is the first moment that Jason has ever succeeded (and could be) proud of himself," Jason's mother said. "I look at autism as the Berlin Wall, and he cracked it."

"As the first shot went in, and then the second shot, as soon as that went in, I just started to catch fire," Jason said. Within days, Jason's achievement was seen around the country, shown on every network and cable news channel and viewed millions of times on internet. The response was immediate and overwhelming.

20 TOTAL POINTS

President George W. Bush met with Jason, making a special trip to an airport near Jason's home to congratulate him on his once-in-a-lifetime game.

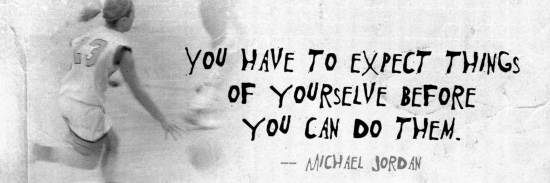

YOU HAVE TO EXPECT THINGS
OF YOURSELVE BEFORE
YOU CAN DO THEM.

— MICHAEL JORDAN

"Our country was captivated by your amazing story on the basketball court; I think it's a story of Coach Johnson's willingness to give a person a chance ... It's a story of a young man who found his touch on the basketball court, which in turn, touched the hearts of citizens all across the country," said President Bush.

Jason won the ESPY Award for the "Best Moment in Sports" in 2006, and his story is being made into a movie. In the meantime, Jason works near his home and travels the country raising awareness for autism, all because Jason seized an opportunity. And in four short minutes, he changed his life—and the lives of countless others.

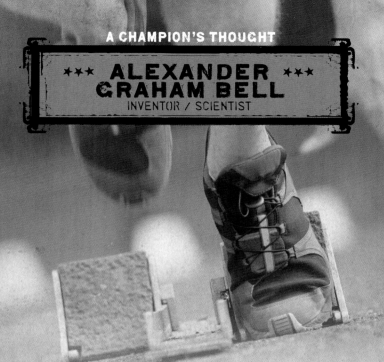

*** **ALEXANDER GRAHAM BELL** ***

INVENTOR / SCIENTIST

When one door closes, another opens,
but we often look so long and so regretfully
upon the closed door that we do not see the
one which has opened for us.

OPPORTUNITY

INTEGRITY

WISDOM IS KNOWING THE RIGHT PATH TO TAKE ... INTEGRITY IS TAKING IT.

— Michael H. McKee

We all make good decisions when someone's watching us. But how many of us will always make the right decision—on the field or on the court, in the classroom, in life—when we're our own judge? **Two critical elements of integrity are truthfulness and honesty. Together, these two core values serve to support your decisions as well as the actions that ultimately define you as a person of integrity.**

Your integrity is the centerpiece of your character. The slightest compromise of your integrity will leave your character flawed in some way. So choose your thoughts, your words and your actions carefully, always staying on the path of integrity.

A true test of your integrity is how you act when no one else is around. You see, your

actions become your habits and your habits become your character and your character becomes your destiny. So, even when there is no one around to impress with your act of integrity, you must always strive to impress yourself, first and foremost.

A CHAMPION ASKS...

 AM I TRULY PROUD OF HOW I RESPONDED TO A DIFFICULT SITUATION?

 WOULD I BE ASHAMED IF I _____ ?

 CAN SOMEONE BE HURT BY MY ACTIONS?

TOM KITE
INTEGRITY
IS NOT A MOVING TARGET

Golf is a sport where athletes are honor-bound to police themselves. So much of golf happens when others aren't looking—a ball stuck deep in the brush or down a path obstructed from view. Even if you've never played golf, you can relate. **Players who spend years and years working their way to the top of their sport are often forced to make difficult decisions that reveal their character and how much they respect their sport and themselves.**

Early in his career, Tom Kite, an up-and-coming golfer, was in contention for his first win on the PGA Tour. Lining up an important birdie putt, Kite accidentally moved his ball—a penalty, even though no one had seen it. Kite called the infraction on himself—and lost the tournament.

"It was the only thing I could do. When you break a rule, you suffer the consequences," Kite said. "I have to live with finishing second for a few days. I have to live with myself for the rest of my life."

Kite would go on to become an elite golfer of his generation—and someone his peers recognized as a keen and honest competitor. Like Tom Kite, you must decide early in your athletic career to honor the rules and limits of your sport—know the right path—and take it.

Rule 18 — Moving the Ball

If you or your partner move either of your balls on purpose or accidentally, add a penalty stroke to your score, replace and play it.

JOHN WOODEN

COLLEGE BASKETBALL COACH, WINNER OF
★★ 10 NCAA CHAMPIONSHIPS IN 12 YEARS ★★

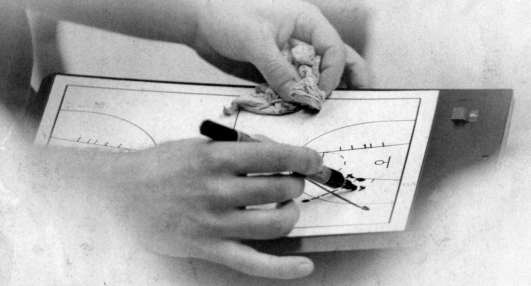

Be more concerned with your character than
your reputation, because your character is what
you really are, while your reputation is merely
what others think you are.

INTEGRITY

THE LOCKER ROOM

By Derek Molis

The mind of an athlete is a powerful weapon. My weapon begins working each time I step into the locker room.

It's a special room, my room, where my pregame rituals always remain the same. It is in this room where I first take a seat on the bench, when I mentally begin preparing myself for the game. I begin with a thought process which tells me there are two kinds of athletes in this world: Athletes who set goals and meet them, and athletes who set goals, but never act on them. Myself, I am an athlete, born and raised. I act on the goals I set for myself! As I begin to undress the layer of life which matters no more, I remind myself how lucky I really am. How lucky I am to have my health. How lucky I am to have been given these abilities to play this game that I love so much. But most of all, how lucky I am to dress myself with pride in the uniform once again. As I lace up my shoes and look around the room, I pray that my teammates have similar thoughts. I pray that they understand the significance of this room, that this is our meeting place. The place where we have shared so many good times, but also helped one another get through the bad. The place where we have come together again to prepare ourselves for another fight of our lives. I have now fine-tuned my weapon, and I am ready to make my goals become reality. I am ready to go out there and play this game as if it were the last game I were ever able to play. I reflect upon one final thought: How thankful I am for the opportunity to once again enter and leave the Locker Room.

— Derek Molis

PURPOSE

STRONG LIVES ARE MOTIVATED BY DYNAMIC PURPOSES.

— Kenneth Hildebrand

PURPOSE IS AN ELUSIVE COMBINATION OF DESIRE, MOTIVATION, AND VISION COUPLED WITH THE ABILITY TO FORGE AHEAD DESPITE THE ROADBLOCKS FACING YOU.

Your purpose helps guide your actions towards your goal. **Without a purpose you can drift aimlessly from task to task**, never accomplishing anything. By establishing your purpose and working backward, you can create small steps that lead you to your purpose.

For example, if you're a senior in high school, then your purpose as a student may be to graduate and go to college. To accomplish this, you will need to direct your daily activities to serve that purpose—go to school, do your homework, get good grades and graduate. As an athlete, what is your purpose: to be a leader, to be a follower, to develop into a world-class athlete? There is no correct answer. Each of us has been put on this earth to serve a unique purpose.

Finally, I believe that being true to your heart and choosing to

serve others are two critical components in anyone's purpose. If you build your foundation of purpose on these two beliefs, then there is nothing that you can't accomplish. No matter what your purpose may be, be true to yourself and let your actions guide you.

A CHAMPION ASKS...

AM I FULLY COMMITTED TO MY PURPOSE?

HOW MIGHT MY PURPOSE CHANGE OVER TIME?

HOW DOES MY PURPOSE ALSO SERVE OTHERS?

PURPOSE

TO BE MORE THAN "ME"

On a normal Saturday night in Milwaukee, Wisconsin, at a high school basketball game that few people would have remembered, purpose was the driving force behind an extraordinary act of sportsmanship and a son's tribute to the memory of a loved one. **Earlier that day, Milwaukee Madison captain Johntel Franklin lost his mother.**

Carlitha Franklin, only 39, had fought and beaten cervical cancer. After a five-year remission, the cancer returned. The same day she was hospitalized, while her son took his college entrance exams, she passed away.

Despite the sudden loss, Johntel went to the gym that evening, where his team would play DeKalb, a team that had driven two-and-a-half hours from Illinois to renew a budding rivalry. Teammates and fans, knowing about Johntel's loss, surrounded him and expressed their sympathies. His team was playing the game only at his insistence.

When Johntel told his coach that he was there to play, not to watch, the coach put him in the game. Coach Aaron Womack, Jr., knew that Johntel was there for a purpose, and he wanted him on the floor.

The only catch: Because Franklin wasn't on the roster for the game—no one thought that he would play, given the circumstances—DeKalb would get to shoot two technical foul shots. It was a close game, and Womack knew that giving away two points could tip the outcome. Still, he didn't care. If, under the most trying circumstances imaginable, his senior captain had come to play, he would play.

DeKalb's Darius McNeal volunteered to take the shots. After discussing the situation with his coach, Dave Rohlman, McNeal intentionally missed both shots, practically dribbling the ball toward the hoop.

The gesture was immediately recognized by everyone in the gym, especially the Milwaukee Madison players and coaches, who stood and applauded the selfless act of sportsmanship and compassion that the DeKalb team had shown for their grieving captain.

"I did it for the guy who lost his mom," McNeal said after the game. "It was the right thing to do."

Johntel went on to score 10 points in a 62-47 win. After the game, the two teams sat down together for pizza and soda.

"This is something our kids will hold for a lifetime," Rohlman said. "They may not remember our record 20 years from now, but they'll remember what happened in that gym that night."

RONALD REAGAN
★ 40TH PRESIDENT OF THE UNITED STATES ★

At this moment, you are in one of the most exciting phases of your life—your teen years. The whole world lies before you. The opportunities are limitless. What you do, where you go, and what you become depends on your willingness to work toward a goal. As an athlete, you have already learned the virtue of perseverance. You have learned that you can overcome obstacles with the proper effort and practice. If you pursue other goals throughout life with the same tenacity, you will succeed. Most importantly, the real key to success is within you. No one can give it to you or take it from you. You hold your destiny in your hands.

PURPOSE

FAITH

FAITH IS COURAGE; IT IS CREATIVE WHILE DESPAIR IS ALWAYS DESTRUCTIVE.

— David S. Muzzey

Athletes are trained to believe in themselves.
Even in team sports, the individual makes the tackle or scores the winning run. You are taught from an early age that confidence breeds success and that to rely on teammates to do your job is a recipe for disaster.

But sometimes, even athletes aren't immune to the events that would challenge the strongest character. How do you overcome these events? The answer? Faith. According to Webster's dictionary faith is defined as, "a firm belief in something for which there is no proof." However, one could argue that faith without a basis is not much different from insanity. Religion, science and hard work serve as building blocks for faith. As an athlete you attempt to build your faith on multiple fronts, with hard work being an essential

IF YOU **THINK** YOU CAN WIN, **YOU CAN** WIN. FAITH IS NECESSARY TO VICTORY.

component. Faith grows stronger when you give your all in practice, the game, training, diet, school, etc. Faith allows you to overcome the fear of failure, to quiet the nagging indecision that might make you miss the game-winning shot or blow the clutch catch.

In the end, faith is ultimately a belief in something greater than yourself, and sometimes it requires you to trust forces outside your control and without any tangible proof of a positive outcome. I challenge you to not only continue to build your faith, but also to have faith.

A CHAMPION ASKS...

 IS MY FAITH GROWING STRONGER?

 HOW CAN I HELP OTHERS GROW THEIR FAITH?

 CAN I RELY UPON MY FAITH?

DARIUS POOLE
FAITH
TO MOVE ON

Darius Poole was one of the lucky ones. In August 2008, the Melrose High School wide receiver was relaxing at home with his family in Orange Mound, a community in Memphis, Tennessee, when their apartment caught fire. Only Darius and a younger brother, De'Andre, escaped. His mother, five siblings, and two cousins did not.

The tragedy drew the community together. Recalling the kind of crowd that Darius might have seen on Friday nights rooting his team on to victory, more than 1,000 people joined him in mourning his family.

Just weeks later, Darius returned to the team, astonishing his teammates with his faith and his tenacity as he recovered from the burns and the psychological scars he carried.

"It's unbelievable," coach Hubbard Alexander said of Darius' return. "I don't see how he can do it. We're not pushing him. He's setting his own pace, and it's like he hasn't missed a beat." In November, Darius scored his first touchdown of the season in a playoff win against rival Brighton. **Every time he scores six, Darius said, he points to the heavens and holds up seven fingers, a tribute to his lost family members and an acknowledgement of his faith.**

With the support of teammates, Darius' return to football—and to life—has been made a little bit easier. But it may have been a visit to the hospital in the aftermath of the tragedy that set Darius on the right path. Coach Justin Terry, who also teaches at Melrose High, comforted Darius in the hours after his loss (both Darius and his brother, Dion, who died in the fire, were students of Terry). "I told him, 'Son, God has something in store for you and your brother (De'Andre) to survive and help your family out,' Terry said. 'There's something in store for you right away.'"

In the life of Darius Poole, faith has a new meaning: trust that things will work out, even after a tragedy so great that beliefs are pushed to the breaking point. Darius found peace through the support of his teammates, coaches and community—and by remembering the joy his family brought to him.

"I think about all the good that they did, the things that just make me smile," he said. "The days I think about it, I just pray." Faith and hard work will get you there, just over the horizon. Sometimes, to **FINISH STRONG**, you have to find a way—or make one.

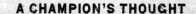

A CHAMPION'S THOUGHT

★★★ **STAN SMITH** ★★★

PROFESSIONAL TENNIS PLAYER, INTERNATIONAL
HALL OF FAME, SIX-GRAND SLAMS, ONE-MAJOR

If we prepare thoughtfully, work hard,
have faith in God's plan for us and are honest with
ourselves, we can most closely reach the perfection
of our talents. By doing this, we can live in peace
with ourselves and our accomplishments.

FAITH

IT'S ALL IN A STATE OF MIND

If you think you are beaten, you are
If you think you dare not, you won't,
If you like to win, but don't think you can
It's almost a cinch you won't

If you think you'll lose, you're lost
For out in the world you find,
Success begins with a fellow's will
It's all in a state of mind

For many a game is lost
Ere even a play is run,
And many a coward fails
Ere even his work is begun

Think big and your deeds will grow
Think small and you'll fall behind
Think that you can and you will
It's all a state of mind

If you think you are out-classed, you are
You've got to think high to rise
You've got to be sure of yourself before
You can ever win a prize

Life battles don't always go
To the stronger or faster man
But sooner or later, the man who wins
Is the fellow who thinks he can.

— Anonymous

DAN GABLE
VISION
BEYOND DEFEAT

Estimates put the snow fall total at nine inches for Waterloo, Iowa. That did not matter to Dan as he threw snow from the shovel faster than any snow blower could match. He was almost done clearing the driveway, and that made him even angrier. He wished that there was more to do. The thoughts of last night's loss were still firing up every nerve ending in his body. Young Dan Gable genuinely hated to lose.

Standing in that clean driveway, he vowed never to lose again.

Dan knew that simply wishing it so would not make it so. And the thing he loved about wrestling was that his efforts would directly impact his reward: winning. So he developed a list of daily goals and then prioritized them in a manner that would support his vision of winning—always. Next, he committed to working his list of priorities; always focusing from the top down and never letting the lower priorities trump the top ones. Dan's philosophy:

"When you finally decide how successful you really want to be, you've got to set priorities. Then, each and every day, you've got to take care of the top ones. The lower ones may fall behind, but you can't let the top ones slip. You don't forget about the lower ones though because they can add up to hurt you. Just take care of the top ones first."

After that snowy day in the driveway—and for the rest of his prep years—he would make good on his promise of never losing again; winning 64 matches in a row, including three state championships.

In the summer before going to college, Dan had the opportunity to workout with Bob Buzzard, an Iowa wrestler whom he admired. As a three-time state champion and undefeated since the snowstorm, Dan was very confident that he could give Bob a run for his money. He was wrong and Bob proceeded to teach Dan a valuable lesson by dominating him on the mat. Dan quickly realized that college wresting was much different from high school.

Realizing that he would have to take his training to a whole new level, Dan recommitted himself to his efforts.

"My vision was clear—State Champion, NCAA Champion and Olympic Champion. To get there I had to set an everyday goal which was to push myself to exhaustion or, in other words, to work so hard in practice that someone would have to carry me off the mat."

Dan reinvented the term "conditioning." He trained every day for six to eight hours. Sometimes, at night, he would wake up and fear that a competitor may be training harder than him so he would jump out of bed and start doing push ups.

His vision of becoming an NCAA Champion was realized his  sophomore year and then again in his junior year. In his senior year, Dan Gable entered the NCAA tournament with an unbelievable record of 177-0. To say he dominated his sport is an understatement. He owned his sport.

Very few doubted that he would march through the tournament once again. And that is exactly what happened—at first. In his first five matches, he pinned all five opponents and only went into the second period one time. But there was one more match to go. In this match, he faced Larry Owings from the University of Washington and Larry had a different plan for the match. You see, Larry recognized that because Dan was so dominate, he rarely had to go the distance with his opponents. Larry believed that if he could get Dan into the third period, he could beat him. And he did. With less than 45 seconds remaining in the match, Larry scored three points and won the match 13-11; handing Dan his first loss since that snowy day in junior high. Dan's record from high school through college was 182-1.

The loss was devastating for Dan. But he stayed true to his vision. The next item on his list was to become an Olympic champion. He rededicated himself to this vision and never looked back.

According to Dan, "Raising your level of performance requires a proper mentality and meaning from within. This gives you the ability and drive to work on the things necessary to go to a higher level. When people ask me how to raise their level of performance, the first thing I ask is, how important is it to you?"

Two years later, his vision was realized. Dan Gable won the gold medal in wrestling, becoming an Olympic champion. Of his 21 matches, he pinned 12 men and outscored the other opponents 130-1 (coincidently losing his only point to Larry Owings). He would move on to become the head coach for the University of Iowa, where he instilled his philosophy of winning into the blood of the wrestling program. During his time as head coach, Iowa won 15 NCAA titles—nine of them consecutively and seven of them to top off perfect seasons. Dan coached for 21 years. During that time, his teams won 94% of the time—a record that stands to this day.

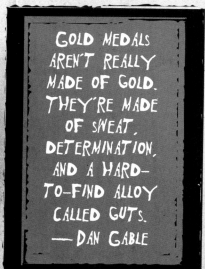

GOLD MEDALS AREN'T REALLY MADE OF GOLD. THEY'RE MADE OF SWEAT, DETERMINATION, AND A HARD-TO-FIND ALLOY CALLED GUTS.
— DAN GABLE

Dan Gable never lost sight of his vision in good times and bad. He stayed focused on his long-term vision and his goals were realized even beyond his own imagination.

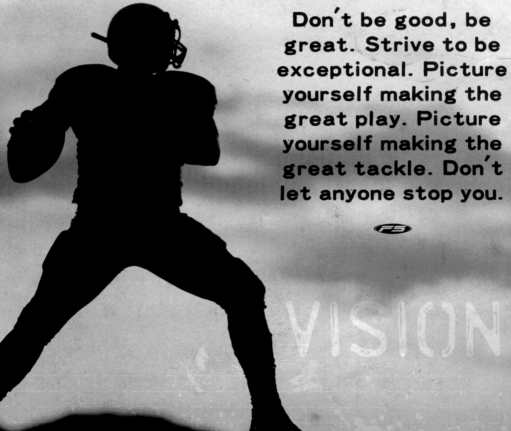

★★ DAN HAMPTON ★★

NFL DEFENSIVE TACKLE/HALL OF FAME, SUPER BOWL CHAMPION AND FOUR-TIME PRO BOWLER

Don't be good, be great. Strive to be exceptional. Picture yourself making the great play. Picture yourself making the great tackle. Don't let anyone stop you.

VISION

DREAM

NOTHING HAPPENS BUT FIRST A DREAM.

— Carl Sandburg

Dreams take a lot of different shapes. In the same way that vision helps you to see your way to the future, dreams offer limitless possibility. Sometimes, dreams allow us to escape, to imagine a better future than the one we find ourselves in. A good rule of thumb:

DREAM BIG, OR NOT AT ALL

But to realize a dream, you have to ask the right questions. If I could accomplish any one thing, what would it be? How do I get there from here? How far can a dream take me? Next, you must visualize your dream as best as you can.

SOME PEOPLE DREAM OF SUCCESS WHILE OTHERS WAKE UP AND ACHIEVE IT. —UNKNOWN

THE ATHLETE'S DREAMLINE PROCESS

1. ASK
THE RIGHT QUESTIONS

2. VISUALIZE
YOUR DREAM

3. REFLECT
ON YOUR WORK

See yourself in your dream reaping the benefits you crave. Imagine what it will feel like when your dream comes true —what do you see, hear, and smell? Then reflect back on all you had to do to realize this dream—the goals, the discipline, the hard work and the feelings of accomplishment. Don't leave anything out. Be as detailed as possible because these images and feelings will serve to anchor you as you work to achieve your dream.

Be warned. Your mind is a very powerful tool. Don't take this exercise lightly, because it can change your life … forever.

A CHAMPION ASKS...

IS MY DREAM
SUPPORTED WITH
GOALS AND
OBJECTIVES?

WHAT CHANGES DO I
NEED TO MAKE TO SET
MY LIFE ON COURSE
FOR ACHIEVING
THIS DREAM?

WHAT RESOURCES
DO I NEED TO HELP ME
GET THERE?

CARL JOSEPH

DREAM

TO BE A CHAMPION

Ask Florida's Carl Joseph. A three-sport star in high school, captain of the football team (and later a player at Bethune-Cookman College), Carl knew better than anyone the value of a dream. **He dreamed that he would jump as high and throw as far as his opponents in track and field. He dreamed that he would dunk a basketball and letter (twice) on his high school team. He dreamed that he would play college football after graduating from high school.** And Carl—friends and admirers called him "Sugarfoot," a reference to his sweet abilities—did all of those things, despite being born with one leg. Carl was born in Madison, Florida, just outside Tallahassee, and grew up on a tobacco farm with nine siblings. "My mama never felt sorry for me, and I never felt sorry for myself," Carl said. "You can do whatever you want to do when your mind is determined. What can stop you?"

When he played, he did so without any prosthesis (you can see a remarkable highlight film of Carl on internet, where he runs down an opposing quarterback from behind). "It just slowed me down," Carl said of his decision to play on one leg. Carl was so dominating on the football field in high school that he earned All-America honors. His single best game? It was against Brooks County, Georgia, when he made 11 solo tackles, intercepted a pass and blocked a punt. And he was being double-teamed by much bigger players for the entire game.

His talents were featured on such television programs as *Today* and *That's Incredible.* Today, Carl is a father of nine and lead singer of Carl Joseph and the Spiritual Tru-Tones. Moreover, he teaches special-needs children and coaches football for the Jefferson County High School team near Tallahassee. In February 2009, Carl was elected to Florida's High School Athletic Hall of Fame.

"I feel really blessed that after all these years an honor like this could happen to me," Carl said. **"When I was a little kid, I used to actually dream about playing varsity sports in high school. But now, to be among these great athletes, that's something I never could've imagined."**

The dream comes home.

A CHAMPION'S THOUGHT

★★★ **LARRY BIRD** ★★★

PROFESSIONAL BASKETBALL PLAYER, THREE-TIME
NBA CHAMPION, THREE-TIME NBA MVP

When I was young,
I never wanted to leave
the court until I got things
exactly correct. My dream
was to become a pro.

PATIENCE

I DIDN'T JUST JUMP BACK ON THE BIKE AND WIN. THERE WERE A LOT OF UPS AND DOWNS, GOOD RESULTS AND BAD RESULTS, BUT THIS TIME I DIDN'T LET THE LOWS GET TO ME.

— Lance Armstrong

Patience is a virtue, the old saying goes, but that doesn't mean that you're content to sit on the bench after putting in thousands of hours chasing a dream. No, having **patience means preparing yourself to make the most of an opportunity when it arises**, balancing your steely-eyed determination to succeed with the knowledge that your hard work and dedication will pay off when the coach calls your number.

True, you must have a long-term vision, but you must also have a perspective that your vision will take time to be realized. Real, sustainable success takes time, practice and patience. Experts agree that the magic number for mastering a skill is 10,000. It takes 10,000 hours of work to reach the pinnacle of your endeavor. There are no short cuts. Be patient, be determined and be willing to put in the work.

THE MAGIC NUMBER
10,000

Patience does not have to be painful. On the contrary, **use your patience to enjoy the process of what you are doing. Take a moment to reflect on your accomplishment after you've finished an exercise.** Embrace that moment in time as a building block in the skyscraper of your vision; knowing that you are one step closer to your goal.

A CHAMPION ASKS...

 DO MY DAILY EFFORTS SUPPORT MY LONG-TERM VISION?

 DO I TAKE TIME TO ENJOY THE PROCESS?

 CAN I BURY FRUSTRATION AND MAINTAIN A LONG-TERM VIEW?

MICHAEL JORDAN
PATIENCE
PREVAILS

Many players might have called it quits if they were told to spend a year on the junior varsity basketball team. For Michael, a gangly kid from Laney High School in Wilmington, North Carolina, who had more faith in his own ability than his coach did, the news that **he hadn't made his high school roster** didn't sit well.

Michael didn't lack confidence in his own abilities—he was an accomplished baseball player and knew that he was even better at basketball—and being placed on the junior varsity squad was certainly a setback in his quest to become a star athlete. **"It was embarrassing not making the team,"** Michael said. **"They posted the roster and it was there for a long, long time without my name on it.** I remember being really mad, too, because there was a guy who made it that really wasn't as good as me. "I think that not making the varsity team drove me to really work at my game, and also taught me that if you set goals,

YOU'RE NEVER A LOSER UNTIL YOU QUIT TRYING.
— MIKE DITKA

and work hard to achieve them—the hard work can pay off."

Instead of letting the decision get him down, though, Michael tempered his dedication to the game with patience, waiting for the right time to make his move. He continued to hone his skills during that long year on the JV squad, averaging 25 points a game and positioning himself to make the varsity team the following season. **"Whenever I was working out and got tired and figured I ought to stop, I'd close my eyes and see that list in the locker room without my name on it,"** he said, **"and that usually got me going again."**

So what came of an athlete's patience and his dedication in the face of adversity? That junior-varsity basketball player was Michael Jordan. After helping the University of North Carolina to the NCAA basketball championship in 1982, he went on to win two Olympic gold medals and six NBA championships. Today, he is recognized as the greatest basketball player ever. His rise to the top of the game began with hard work—and the patience to know that he would make the most of his shot when the time came.

MICHAEL JORDAN

PROFESSIONAL BASKETBALL PLAYER, SIX-TIME NBA
CHAMPION, FIVE-TIME MVP, 14 TIME NBA ALL-STAR

If you're trying to achieve, there will be roadblocks,
I've had them; everybody has had them. But obstacles
don't have to stop you. If you run into a wall, don't
turn around and give up. Figure out how to climb it,
go through it, or work around it.

PATIENCE

NOW IT'S UP TO YOU!

As you see, the **FINISH STRONG** mindset is not singular in nature. To be a true **FINISH STRONG** champion, you must incorporate many core values into your lifestyle, with each value playing a unique role in the success of your efforts.

Having a vision without a purpose will do you no good. Likewise, having a purpose without goals is futile and setting goals without making a commitment is simply an empty promise to yourself. In the end you, and only you, can respond to the challenges in your life. Don't become a victim. **Choose to become a champion.**

When you look back on these formative years, you will realize what a small period in time they represent as it relates to your entire time on earth. **Don't rush your life away.** Have the patience and vision to take each day as it comes. Set your goals, complete your tasks and remember, "Inch by inch life's a cinch; yard by yard life is hard."

Enjoy the ride and most of all **FINISH STRONG**!

FINISH STRONG

ONLINE BONUS CONTENT!

If you would like to learn more about the stories in this book, watch videos of the people featured or share your own Finish Strong story visit:

SIMPLETRUTHS.COM/FSTEEN

Download your FREE goal setting guide today.

REACH YOUR GOALS TOMORROW!

ABOUT THE AUTHOR

Dan Green is an entrepreneur with a passion for finishing strong in everything he does. Over the past 20 years, he has excelled in business and life in large part to his adoption of the **"Finish Strong"** attitude. He currently serves as Executive Vice President and partner with Simple Truths and is also the founder of Finish Strong, LLC.

Dan is the author of three inspirational books; *Finish Strong, Finish Strong Teen Athlete* and *Finish Strong Motivational Quotes.* Collectively his books have been purchased by more than 250,000 people worldwide. The first **Finish Strong** book was used by Drew Brees and the New Orleans Saints as a guiding theme during the 2009 season and ultimately their first Super Bowl victory.

In 1996, Dan trademarked the words **"Finish Strong"** with the intent to inspire the world. Since that time, he has been the

evangelist for spreading its powerful message to individuals across the globe. As a result, thousands of people from all walks of life have made a positive change in their life by embracing the **Finish Strong** attitude as their own personal platform for achievement—in life, sport and business.

Dan lives outside of Chicago, is married and the father of two amazing girls. He enjoys playing the guitar, golfing, boxing, fitness and motorsports.

For more information about Dan, to inquire about speaking engagements, or to learn more about incorporating **Finish Strong** into your next event, visit www.FinishStrong.com or send an email to ContactDan@finishstrong.com.

www.finishstrong.com